Black girl magic
& other elixirs

by
shantell hinton hill

YELLOW ARROW

PUBLISHING

Baltimore, Maryland, USA

Contents

this collection is dedicated to all the Black girl nerds turned boss women who are still working to free the awkward little girl inside of them. i am you and you are me. thank you to my husband, Jeremy, for cheering for me through all the rejections. thank you to my mom who introduced me to my self and my love for reading and writing. thank you to my parents and grandparents who gave me the world and dared me to change it for the good. thank you to my baby girl, Sophie June, who continues to challenge me to show up fully and love my self, regardless.

Black girl magic & other elixirs is an homage to all Black girls and Black women and how we are present and stand up to a world dominated by interlocking oppressions. you can find information about some of the souls herein at the end of this collection.

BLACK GIRL MAGIC
& OTHER ELIXIRS

Black girl magic

i learned how to vanish
into thin air
when i was little.
a witch taught me—
made me do it
because she couldn't stand
the sight of me.

her nickname was Barbie
but i called her Devil
for all the ways
she made me believe
it was alright to hate me
all while she loved my daddy.
guess she was good
at playing pretend,
like her name,
that i could make
my self at home
in the living hell
she created.

on those weekend visits
i perfected the craft
of shrinking my self
until i was invisible
and i recited the spell
so many times
i could say it without thinking—
"i'm sorry, i didn't mean . . ."
to speak.
to laugh.
to exist
in her presence.

so, i excused my self
from taking up space
in her lair.
kept my self safe
by becoming unmentionable
because my silence
always worked
like a charm.

i'm every woman

it was third grade
when i finally discovered
the lyrics of my favorite song
were an incantation
to ward off evil
pale-faced women.

sitting in the back
of Momma's '92 honda accord
we'd ride with the windows down
whisking from grocery store to church
singing our secular tune
that carried sacred wisdom—
gospel to my prepubescent hearing—
which was weighed down
by poisonous words
hanging on me like earrings
from the teacher
who'd never had
a Black girl
like me.

queue song, "I'm Every Woman"

danger and fear
were the twin demons
that had replaced
the grace and mercy
pastor always preached about
and they followed me
into the schoolhouse
everyday—

scolding me
with scalding hot words
that burned a fire inside of me.
"you'll never be able to spell
at the rate you're going"—
she embarrassed me
in front of class one day.
and the flames grew
and grew in me
the burning desire
to cast a spell
she would never
recover from.

so, naturally
i signed my self up
for the school talent show
where i performed
the incantation
that Whitney and Chaka
gave me words to
and waited patiently
for something magical
to happen.

only my pale-faced teacher
was surprised when it did.
because that bit of spellwork
conjured up the warrior
living inside my momma
when she appeared outta thin air
up at my school

to get the teacher and principal
on the same page
of understandin’
and get me outta class for the day—
assuring me that Mrs. Pale-face
would never f*ck with me again.

from that day forward,
i knew.
that every woman
i ever needed
was inside of me
and Momma and Whitney, too.

hide and never seek

"nah-nah-nee boo-boo
you never found me."
was my favorite refrain
every time my big brother
and older cousins
couldn't find my
hiding place.
because i was the best
at hiding.

little did i know
they laughed at my jubilation
because they never looked for me,
the little girl that pestered them.
they only pretended to play along
because they wanted me
to hide for as long
as i could stand it
so they could be free
of me.

after while, i caught on—
the ruse was no longer amusing
and i refused to participate
in the game that
only i was playing.

but, somehow,
my little self
never got the memo
to erase the muscle memory
of how to play
hide and never seek.

i didn't know it
till i was visited by
the five-year-old me
that lodged her self
deep into the darkest place
she could find,
so she could be free
of the feelings
and the fear
she could not control—
from the people bigger than her
who were supposed to keep her safe
but created a charade instead.

and she played along
because they wanted to pretend
everything was okay,
as if they couldn't stand
to see the truth
staring back at them
from the innocent
gleam in my eyes.

so i turned the lights off
behind those eyes
and buried her in the dark
to hide her from the adults
that couldn't bear
to handle
the demons that pestered them.

and, still.
when she finally emerged
from that hiding place—
even after all this time—
she recited the same refrain
she sang so long ago:
"nah-nah-nee boo-boo
you never found me."

only this time
she cried
for all the times
she had to hide
and no one
ever came
looking for her.

how it feels to be free

it's a wonder
that any of us—
raised in Black homes
wit Black mommas, daddies, grannies,
granddaddies, aunties, and uncles 'nem—
know how it feels to be free.

between whoopings
and Sunday School,
we weren't allowed to do much
except what we were told—
get somewhere and sat down
turn them lights off
shut up when grown folks talking
eat these leftovers if you ain't got no McDonald's money
be seen, not heard.

but, sometimes,
we managed to slip between
the fingers of their protective grasp
and find our selves in portals of fantasy
drinking potions of laughter
breaking the sound barrier
with our racket
gliding over asphalt
on the magic roller skates
that showed us how freedom felt
as it slapped against our faces
and flapped our barrettes
in the wind.

it's a wonder we ever came back home
after losing all the manners
punished into us
for those few precious moments
where we made room for our selves
to know how it feels to be free.

shower caps and sandboxes

my first experience
of sand between my toes
was a trip to the sandbox
on the shoreline of the playground
at Harlan Park Christian Childcare Center.

there i was
the only Black fly
buzzing around the sea
of milk white faces
when my teacher reminded me loudly
"don't forget your mom sent your cap!"

but it wasn't a swim cap
my momma wanted me to wear
or even a wide-brimmed, straw hat
to block out the sun.
nope—it was a damn shower cap.

an embarrassingly regular shower cap
that she made me wear
to protect my hair
from the granules of sand
she was tired of plucking
outta my scalp before washing.

the shower cap
never did protect
much else
from the laughing stares
coming from the white faces
with sand blonde hair

"why do you have that thing on?"
they sneered and pointed
at the ridiculous plastic
i wished i could turn
into a teflon shield
to deflect their gaze

"because my momma says it protects my hair."
i answered with my chest
though my heart was in my throat
and my acceptance
sifted through their pale hands
like it was quicksand.

"how come your hair needs protectin'?"
they wondered.
"mine don't,"
they compared.
as if they had never noticed my hair
the way i noticed theirs.

"because my hair is like velcro—
things stick to it."
i explained.
"your hair is like a slip 'n slide,
so things slide out."
they nodded in envy.

and i began to feel
my self
relax under the weight
of their captivation
and settle into the truth
that this was me.

the gangly, Black girl
who wore shower caps
on the playground
because her momma
ain't care nothin' bout
what the white kids was doing.

the irony
of it is funny now.
that they would wish
to wear the same cap
i had been so desperate to
bury in the sand.

but if i had
i would never have been able
to go back for it like this—
the treasure that it is.
the moment in time
i discovered being Black
was one of the best things
about me.

what our little girls are made of

ca. the '90s era

treasure–
unboxing my kenya doll with her kente hammer pants.
flexing–
boxed perms that were just for me and left my hair long and wavy.
snacking–
wavy lays and red jungle juice from the corner store.
wearing–
multicolored knee shorts that made it easy to loopty-loop the bars
on the jungle gym.
walking–
underneath the gym bleachers to go to the concession stand at my
brother's basketball game.
standing–
in a circle of four, playing the down by the rollercoaster game while
we slapped hands.
lathered–
my legs in the cocoa butter or suave lotion covering my hands.
covered–
by Momma's prayers and a little bit of spice.
spicing–
the world i created when only i was watching.
watching–
all the little blonde girls be treated like sugar.
treating–
my self as a treasure, anyway.

liquid sunflowers:
an ode to Momma's perfume

on my mother's dresser
existed a treasure
secretly waiting for me.

and if i was good
i knew Momma would
leave it just in my reach.

so i'd wait by her door
sitting on the floor
watching her adorn her frame.

with a high-waisted skirt
and a shoulder padded shirt
humming a tune that Whitney sang.

then after a short fuss
of eye shadow makeup
and blush and red lipstick

she'd put on her jewels
repeat her one rule
and give me the chance to pick

there were so many perfumes
from which i could choose
but i always wanted just one.

and behind the other glass vials
it sat there reflecting my smile
waiting for me to come.

"you pick that one everytime."
"you said the choice was mine."
we'd laugh at each other in jest.

then she'd spray two puffs
right under her sleeve cuffs
then rub her wrists on her neck.

and there it was yet again
the sweet smell i called friend
all was so right in my world.

because i gained all my powers
from liquid sunflowers
that i inhaled as a girl.

Momma's secret power

i'll never know how she did it
but Momma could always
make my insides feel cozy
like soft, lavender velvet—
like waking up in the mornings
to a toasty house
warmed by the oven
she had opened before we rose
and woke up to the understanding
that she was making a dollar outta
fifteen cents
scraping and saving her coins
and our souls, blessing us
with homemade pancakes
thick as hot-water cornbread
so we'd stay full longer
and remain obliviously content
with our empty pockets
but satisfied bellies.

aunties be knowin'

on everything—
aunties be knowin'
a little something about everything.
about life.
about loss.
about love.
about lust.
about laughter.
about everything.

and in between knowin' all the things
she still be making time
to show up carrying the plate she cooked.
to be your secret carrier.
to care for the parts of you don't nobody else care for.
to carpool your stuff
that you couldn't carry
because she got room
for everything.

like somewhere—
on her way to womanhood,
she learned how to be everywhere,
everytime,
and how to say all the names of everyone
you would ever be.
all because you call her auntie.
and that's her everything.

sister Mary Clarence

brown and white Marias
introduced me to the classic story on the west side
that had a sound like music.
but nothing felt like music
until i met sister Mary Clarence
who had a Black habit of seeing Black kids
as special enough to be somebody.
she was the first teacher I ever had
that introduced me to my self
and instructed me to love her
and inspired me
to wake up
and pay attention
to the musical
within.

on the holy

in the still
of saturday mornings
waking up to the sound of the trumpets.
from the mass of the Mississippi
to angelic tunes of Whitney.
And Anita.
And Nina.

under the unctioning of Mahalia
leading us to precious Lord
taking Her hand
we are fearless,
more than conquerors,
warriors, Black and beautiful
daughters of Jerusalem.

She tells the truth and shames the devil.
Her strength is in the thickness of her thighs.
like Maya, Her words are as leaven
praying over us, still we rise.
new life from Grandma's seasoning
multiplying catfish and cornbread loaves
we come to love our bodies
and lavish our souls.

we know Her as Sophia.
the color purple with the sassy lip.
Her audacity cures—Her courage carries
past the threshold of demons
in white hoods
who colored God's eyes blue.
and permed and painted Her hair yellow.
knowing damn well
both were Black.

so we hear Her
in the rhythm of double dutch ropes.
we see Her
moving across the sea of generations
when She plaits the hair of Her daughters.
and, especially, we feel Her.
we feel Her presence
as power in the room,
prayer languages we never learned,
and a proximity to God only the holy could survive.

God, our mother-auntie-sistafriend

Jesus called God father
because that's what God was
to Him.

it makes sense
since Mary came up pregnant
so magically.

that paternity
would have to be explained
some kinda way.

God being
Jesus' father—
works.

but God
being that for everyone
ain't true.

not all the ways
God's being
looks.

or feels to us
who know God
as something else.

God is
just like Momma
God raised us.

God be
keeping us
like auntie 'nem.

and God
stay freeing us
like that sistafriend.

so, as for me—
i'ma call God
what God is.

if God so loved the world

if God so loved the world,
that God gave us God's Son—
so that by believing
we may have eternal life,
who is it that God loves so much,
that God would give us so many begotten sons
and daughters
and children?
those born to single mothers,
with melanin tans
and negroid skin,
bombed on the borderlands of Gaza
or baked on streets of Ferguson.

does God truly love the whole world?
or just the pieces of it that are washed in white?
parts flowing with milk and honey
easily funneled to offshore accounts.
what part of God
are we to believe in
when God's beloved still perish
via crucifixion
by bullets covered in badges
or cloaked in colonization?
signed in God's name
stamped with the seal
of love for country.

why is it that God's sovereignty
can be proprietary
only for those in power?
fashioned into a yoke
to commodify the oppressed.

convincing us that our struggles
bind us together in "righteousness."
so that we would then turn blind eye
to the bloodied begotten sons
and daughters
and children who are unchosen.
yet, are still God's creation.

how are we to remain
loyal to a God
whose loyalty is limited
to a Bloodline?
who overlooks
the lines of blood
in the dirt
the same soil that houses the ancestors
of both Jew & Gentile.
how are we to love a God
whose love for the world
included a heavenly position for our colorless souls
but not earthly protection for Black & brown bodies?

perhaps we've misread the fine print
of the contract God bought us with.
for it's hard to imagine
a God who calls us into blind complicity
before calling us into beloved community.
because if it was love
that let God's Son be killed
to bring us back to God.
then, maybe these massacres befalling us
is God calling us back to one another.
maybe each dying breath
is God begging us to believe there is a better way.

the ugly sticks

what happens to the ugly stick
that everybody used to hit with
when we were kids
on the playground
waging wars
with words?

"so—
that's why you look like you
been beat with the ugly stick!"
was hurled at the heads
of the chubby,
the dark,
the nappy,
like grenades
when feelings got hurt.
neverminding the carnage
that set in when everyone pointed
and laughed at the target
who believed it to be true.

and, perhaps,
after the years blew by
like the wind
those that lost those playground battles
were able to escape full-blown destruction
by wielding their weapons or shields
but what remains
is the ugly stick
that stuck to them
like shrapnel
that couldn't

be dislodged
from their bodies.

(un)beknownst to them
those painful shards
were contagious—
highly transmissible
across generations.
as if the ugly stick
itself had beat them
to their healing
and headed it off at the pass.
so much so,
that babies believed
they were ugly, too,
without even being told.
or roasted.
or wagered in a war.
where every manner of ugly sticks.

true love weights

we all sat there
on those padded pews
in our little padded bras
underneath the white dresses
they told us to wear.

being called up front
one by one
with our parents
right behind us
they were the reason we'd come.

and after those weeks
of being talked at
about abstinence
we signed a pledge
made a promise so sweet.

then slid a gold ring
on our left ring fingers
to seal the commitment
that we'd wait for true love
before pursuing sexual things.

the only thing left
was to find our selves
in the pursuit of excellence
since "he who findeth a wife"
never seemed to find us

years came and went
and we still sat there
prayed up in those pews
underneath the cloak of purity
they promised would earn us men.

and after all that time
of talking to God
about marriage
men pursued their pleasure
and we'd missed all the signs.

so we slid into dms
with empty ring fingers
to steal the commitment
and secure our true love
from him after him after him.

only to be left
with resentment he built
while we built businesses
and corporations and whole lives
that miraculously found us—

found us truly in love with who we'd become.

the train tracks through my living room

there is a train track through my living room
that separates two worlds
infinities apart.
and i never understood
how they both fit
into one place
called my body.

the one world filled with books and dreams,
while the other brimmed with survival and wit—
these hemispheres only collided
when they came together
to birth me.
i guess that's why i've always felt
like a venn diagram.

never quite understanding the fullness
of my intersections.
desperately trying to hide one half
of my self
from the other.
afraid my native tongue
would give it all away.

i hated those train tracks
that forced me to ask why
my momma folks on this side of town
lived different than my daddy folks
on the other side
of the same town.
too young to know the tracks weren't to blame.

strange meat

daddy jokes about bologna—
says he'll never eat again.
because he ate it so much
as a poor, Black boy
in segregated Mississippi
that the taste of it
makes him sick now.

so he ignores it completely,
acts as if it doesn't exist,
and casts the memory into forgetfulness.
he learned this magic, too,
as a poor, Black boy
in segregated Mississippi
when he stumbled upon a lynched body.

the imagery
of the mangled, Black limbs
hanging there lifeless
would be ushered into oblivion
by the women who raised him
because they knew
what it would do to him
if he re-membered.

and they showed him how
to pack the trauma away
like strange meat
that had sat out in the heat
too long
and the taste of it
would only make him sick.

bland, Sandra Bland

Sandra Bland's name
is always a reminder—
that if she'd stayed meek and docile
like salt that lost its flavor,
that if she'd acted her name out
like a game of charades,
she'd probably still be alive.

now we #sayhername
as a reminder
of what happens
when we just keeping saying their names
instead of saving their lives.
be bland, Sandra Bland.
so this shit don't happen again.

abracadabra ain't never worked for me

abracadabra ain't never worked for me
it only made sense in make believe
cuz here i was saying it with all my might
but nothin' i ever asked for came into sight
i even added it into my nightly prayers
thinking that God would give it extra layers
of the miracle-working power the preachers used to shout
but i guess it was a language God ain't know nothin' bout
cuz of all the things i prayed and wished
nothing ever changed one bit
our tiny little basic house never turned into a castle
my teachers never stopped treating me like a hassle
not one of my problems were ever solved
and not once was my name ever called
i never won no prizes or got my own way
i guess abracadabra was only meant for white folx to say

first and forever homegirl

she drove us everywhere
during the summers—
to popeyes,
then family video
to get a movie to watch
for our sleepover,
and finally back home.
she was my first homegirl
and best, at that.

when we made it back to her house,
we'd pop us some popcorn
in the old school machine
melt butter in the microwave
to pour over the fresh kernels
and pop the vhs into the vcr
on top of the television
sitting next to the window unit
blowing cool air
to ease the Mississippi
heat.

so, i'd sit on her old couch
eating the homemade buttered popcorn
laughing and laughing
till my sides hurt,
then dressing for bed
and joining her in her room
where she sat in her chair
with her housecoat
and rollers on
just waiting for me to finish
the movie she let me pick.

"you finished wit yuh picture, guhl?"
she'd always say
i'd nod my yes ma'am
with the biggest smile
and crawl into the nook on the side
where my granddaddy used to sleep—
before she evicted him for his sleeptalking—
and i'd take my place,
as her most prized guest,
in the most comfortable
queen-sized bed
in the cluttered-est, coziest room
full of wigs and jewelry and peppermints.

we'd stay up half the night
talking and joking and laughing
at the same stories i'd heard before—
the family lore that grew more intricate
the older i got
or the harder i listened.
and after my eyes got too heavy
to stay open for the show and tell
of all the stuff she'd rummaged through her drawers
to find
even though she wasn't looking for nothin',
i'd drift off, as on a smooth sail,
listening to her pray
the Lord's prayer
kneeling down
on her knees
in the home
i came to
as a girl

and met my forever homegirl
whose hugs felt like the entire world.

thank you for loving me with the best love i've ever known, Grandma.
take your rest now. love, your forever homegirl.

cotton fields, time travels

way down in the Delta
right there off highway 49
there is a portal to another dimension
that transports me to another time
the moment I see
the rows of cotton bolls
overgrown and silently
waiting for the ghosts
of my ancestors
to pick and sort and stuff
it into bags
they would never be
fairly paid to carry.

every row of cotton field
that whooshes past my window
whispers the stories
Granny used to tell
of how she got up befo' dawn
walked alluh 'dem miles to the fields
and picked that stuff till it was too dark to see
and how they'd sometimes sing songs
to help pass the time
in the heat
as they labored
for free.

i guess the songs they sang
were so powerful
that these cotton fields
transformed into doorways
affixed to the past time
we have yet to be free of

because their voices
still linger
like the stickiness in the heat
and i hear them calling
out to me—
always the soundtrack
to my time travels—
begging me to remember
to come back home.

get out the galaxy, Black girl

seem like
everybody stuck
on this little thing
called gravity.

constantly
pulling us down
to earth
keeping us.

around the way
on the block
or grounded
in the ghetto.

where sirens
are drowned out
by deep voices
dripping in our silence.

and girls
are only mini women
walking dead-end streets
paved for us.

all while
we train our
necks to fulcrum
our heads to the sky.

to ignore
catcalls and insults
and overlook
the indignity of their desire.

because we
know the sky
ain't all there is
to see here.

so we'll just
keep on walking
with our own secret
headed to another galaxy.

full
of worlds
where we are
already free.

free B.G.

i wonder if she's over there
behind bars
saying "ain't i a damn woman?"
or asking her self
if their bars
are any different
from the ones the ashies spit
over here, on the corner,
on the internet
every damn day.
whether nine years
or 280 characters—
the sentences
all come out the same.
"she didn't follow the rules—
so, she deserves to pay"
the price of admission
to the very machine
y'all love to hate.
B.G. is she
and she is we—
all of us
who been being
policed,
underpaid,
overlabored,
standing tall
yet, still coming up short
waiting on the brothers—
hell, anybody—
to come free us,
instead of coming for us.

free B.G.
free Brittney Griner.
free Black girls.
free Black gays.
free them all.
we all
gone stay locked up
unless we get free
together.

it must be magic, really

when yellow-haired girls
go missing,
the whole world stops
and watches
in horror—
praying for their safe return.

when Black-bodied girls
go missing,
no one even knows
they've vanished
into nothingness—
like they was nothing to nobody.

it must be magic.
white magic, that is.
to trick people
into not noticing
when a whole human
disappears.

because it just can't be
anything else
besides magic
that materializes who matters
into matter for the media—
just not Black girls' lives.

we only matter
as antimatter.
galactic memories
cast into cauldrons
of forgetfulness
it must be magic, really.

to be forgotten
before we are ever found
misplaced
never re-membered
a figment in
our own imaginations.

Morrison's whisper

there is a palpable,
hypnotic gathering
found in Morrison's whisper.
escaping effortlessly
from her poised pen
and into pages filled with Black
beyond the pale.
so powerful,
that even her spoken words
softly confront
the white gaze
who know nothing
about the margins
where the characters
live the scripted lives
she gave them.

*thank you, Mrs. Morrison, for showing us the way back to our selves
and creating spaces where we are centered and belong. i will never
forget the power exuded in your whisper.*

Venus and Serena

hair beads as body armor,
dawned on their braided crowns
these goddesses walked among us
gripping us with their sound.

singing sounds of the mighty
when they swung racket to ball
we listened to their war cry
as they made opponents fall.

they glided, galloped, and grunted
showing their intensity out loud
with every Black household watching
making all the little Black girls proud.

they were so other-worldly
but belonged to us all the same.
their brown skin and muscular builds
gave permission to our curvy frames.

their power was something to marvel—
only rivaled by their confidence and sass.
never once did they stumble or waver
but wore their audacity with class.

these sisters are something like saviors,
redeeming us from narratives we never wrote.
giving us platforms to new podiums
and placing trophies in our hands to hold.

*thank you, Venus and Serena, for your hard work and bravery. thank
you for giving little Black girls with boisterous attitudes space to be
who we are.*

ontology: a Black woman's requiem

we have turned weapons into plowshares
tilled soils on distant shores
we created culture out of nothing
and forged new life out of wars.

we led the way as vanguards
parting the oppressive seas.
we pressed our way through terror
and still became all we could be.

we birthed generation after generation
and generated thriving for our selves.
we quilted patterned covers of softness
to store upon our wearied souls' shelves.

we came and saw about one another
saving our selves from the throes of debt.
we lavished our selves in our own love
because we knew we could do it best.

we planted our feet where we fell,
though we stumbled time after time.
and we stood back up, firmly rooted
determined to make it to starshine.

we have always been more than our trauma
far greater than mere survivors of life—
for we are the vanquishers of death
who make magic out of our strife.

starshine and clay

starshine is not afraid of darkness
and clay is not afraid of contortion
that's why we know them well.

we span our selves between them
journeying from place to place
borrowing truths along the way.

becoming whatever we knead
emitting light into the vastness
of lands spoken in prophecy.

conforming freedom into clay bricks
starshining new worlds aglow in the darkness—
we celebrate what we have built:
lives we long to live.

yes, i will celebrate

yes, i will celebrate
the many lives i've lived
from ancestor to progeny
the fact still remains
i am here
shifting
shaping
shape-shifting in my hands
the kind of world i want to give
to my daughter(s).
one where she will marvel
at her own glory
far before she is praised
for her gifts.
a place where the soil
nurtures every seed
and bears every fruit
under the suns.
yes, i will celebrate
and sing loudly
for that day to come.
making notes
unseen
become the substance
of soul melodies—
rhythms carried
in our bloodstreams
from here to eternity.

starshine child

promise me, starshine child,
that you will leave
constellations for me in the sky.

so that i can know, starshine child,
you are lighting up worlds
bright as the gleam in your eye.

i won't be able to go, starshine child.
my job was only to dream
and give them to you to shape.

so i bundled 'em all, starshine child,
handed you blueprints of hope unseen
eager to see what you'd make.

now you flying high, starshine child,
mapping new universes
like our ancestors foretold.

make us proud, starshine child,
build beauty out of the clay
only you can mold.

say their names:
the girls and women behind the poetry

poetry is an exercise in communal meaning-making and storytelling. and many poems in this collection have been influenced by actors, athletes, matriarchs, writers, and more. here is a brief overview of the people and moments that coalesced into the content of these poetic offerings. the information follows the order of the poems within.

****

"i'm every woman" celebrates the incredible song of the same name released and sung by Chaka Khan (on her debut album *Chaka* from 1978) then covered by Whitney Houston in 1992.

sister Mary Clarence, mentioned in the poem of the same name, is the protagonist, played by Whoopi Goldberg, from the 1992 and 1993 hit films, *Sister Act 1* and *Sister Act 2: Back in the Habit.*

the women mentioned in "on the holy": Whitney Houston, Anita Baker (legendary singer/songwriter), Nina Simone (classically trained pianist and the Queen of Soul), Maya Angelou (author, poet, and foremother of Black women's artistry), and Sophia (character in *The Color Purple*).

"if god so loved the world" was originally published in July 2022 at shantellhhill.com.

"ugly sticks" addresses how Black girls see themselves. in 2020, on instagram live, a four-year-old Black girl named Ariana told her loctician she was ugly, and it went viral. this poem is a response to all the little Arianas, both alive and/or living inside of us, who have believed or have been told that they were ugly.

"true love weights" refers to a popular evangelical, Christian curriculum entitled "true love waits" that teaches sexual purity before marriage.

Sandra Bland from "bland, Sandra Bland" is a Black American daughter, activist, and truth-teller who was found hanging in a jail cell in Texas in 2015. she was pulled over for a minor traffic violation. no one has been charged in her death.

"free B.G." references Brittney Griner, a prolific Black American basketball player who was detained and imprisoned in Russia for minor drug-related offenses.

"Morrison's whisper" references an interview where acclaimed author, Toni Morrison, responds to journalist Jana Wendt's question about including white subjects in her writing. the interview was from 1998 for the program "Toni Morrison: Uncensored," addressing topics such as her Nobel Prize and racism.

Venus and Serena Williams (from "Venus and Serena") are tennis champions who recently retired from the sport after years of dominance across the world.

poems that reference Lucille Clifton's "won't you celebrate with me" are "ontology: a Black woman's requiem," "starshine and clay," "yes, i will celebrate," and "starshine child." "starshine and clay" is a direct tribute to Lucille Clifton.

the line "a place where the soil" from "yes, i will celebrate" pays homage to a quote in the opening chapter of *The Bluest Eye* (1970) by Toni Morrison: "This soil is bad for certain kinds of flowers . . ."

shantell hinton hill is the ultimate Renaissance woman.

an engineer turned pastor, shantell situates her work at the intersections of social justice, public theology, and Black feminism/womanism. a native of Conway, Arkansas, shantell is married to Rev. Jeremy Hill. they recently welcomed their first child, Sophie June, to their growing family. shantell obtained a master of divinity from Vanderbilt Divinity School. she also earned a bachelor of science in electrical engineering from Vanderbilt University and a master of science in electrical engineering from Colorado State University.

she is a proud member of Delta Sigma Theta Sorority, Inc., and the National Society of Black Engineers. she is also an ordained minister in the Christian Church (Disciples of Christ). her vocational experiences include work as a process control engineer, a Bible teacher, and as Assistant University Chaplain at Vanderbilt. at Winthrop Rockefeller Foundation, shantell focuses on community engagement, faith-based coalition building, and narrative change to imagine more just communities in Arkansas. in her spare time, shantell is also a freelance writer/author and curates digital content that centers on wholeness and thriving.

Thank you for supporting independent publishing.

Yellow Arrow Publishing is a nonprofit supporting writers and artists identifying as women. Visit YellowArrowPublishing.com for information on our publications, workshops, and writing opportunities.